Homes around the world

Island homes

Nicola Barber

WAYLAND

First published in Great Britain in 2006 by Wayland,
an imprint of Hachette Children's Books

Copyright © 2006 Wayland

Hachette Children's Books
338 Euston Road, London NW1 3BH

Editor: Hayley Leach
Senior Design Manager: Rosamund Saunders
Designer: Elaine Wilkinson
Geography consultant: Ruth Jenkins

Printed and bound in China

British Library Cataloguing in Publication Data
Barber, Nicola
  Island home. - (Homes around the world)
  1.Dwellings - Juvenile literature 2.Islands -
  Juvenile literature
  I.Title
  643.1'09142

ISBN-10: 0-7502-4870-x
ISBN-13: 978-0-7502-4870-9

Cover photograph: a group of colourful houses on
an island off Norway.

Photo credits: Bruno Morandi/Robert Harding Picture
Library/Getty 6, Karin Slade/Getty Images 7, Paul
Chesley/Getty Images 8, Ron Chapple/Getty Images 9,
Robert Harding Picture Library Ltd/Alamy 10 and 27,
Pat Shearman/Alamy 11, Nagelestock.com/Alamy cover
and 12, Anders Ryman/Corbis 13 and 23, Craig
Lovell/Eagle Visions Photography/Alamy 14, Ryan
McVay/Getty Images 15, Jean Pragen/Getty Images 16
and 26, Neil Cooper/Alamy 17, Matthieu Paley/Getty
Images 18, Chloe Harford/Corbis 19, Jeremy
Hoare/Alamy 20, Joson/zefa/Corbis 21, Colin
Prior/Corbis 22, Colin Prior/Getty Images 23, Scottish
Viewpoint/Alamy 24, Dinodia/Alamy 25.

Contents

Words in **bold** can be found in the glossary on page 28

What is an island home?

An island is a piece of land that is surrounded by water. There are islands all over the world. Some people live on small islands that lie close to a larger piece of land, called the **mainland**.

▼ *Mont Saint Michel island is near to the mainland of France.*

Some islands are very big. For example, the country of Japan is made up of four large islands – and more than three thousand small islands! The British Isles has over 6,000 islands.

▲ *Japan is an island. Tokyo in Japan is one of the largest cities in the world.*

Big and small islands

Lots of people live and work on islands. Some of them have homes in big cities which are often crowded. Many people live on islands, far from other land, where there are not many people.

Island life
Some islands are so small that no-one lives on them at all!

▲ *Manhattan Island in New York has tall buildings for homes and offices.*

Some islands are tiny, such as the Maldives in the Indian Ocean. There are 1,190 of these islands, but if you add up the land they cover it is just 300 **square kilometres** (sq km). The largest island in the world is Greenland which covers 2,166,086 sq km.

▲ *These homes are on the tiny island of Cebu, in the Philippines.*

Hot and cold islands

In hot places, people sometimes build their houses on **stilts**. The stilts raise the house up off the ground. The air underneath keeps the house cool. The stilts also help to stop snakes and other animals coming into the house!

▼ *This house on Flores, Indonesia has windows with gaps between wooden bars to let air inside.*

In places where the weather is wet
and windy, houses are often built of stone.
The stone walls keep the rain and wind out.
Inside, the house is dry and warm.

Island life

In many places, people make the
roofs of their houses out of grass.
This is known as thatch.

▲ This house
in the Outer
Herbides has
small windows
to stop it
losing heat.

Building an island home

People use a wide variety of **materials** to build their island homes. In large cities tall buildings are made from **concrete**, **steel** and glass. In small villages people often build their houses from wood.

▼ *These brightly painted wooden houses are on an island in Norway.*

Because islands are often far away from other places, homes are often made from **local** materials. People use stones to build the walls of houses, or **bricks** made out of earth.

▲ *This woman on the Pacific island of Satawal is using leaves to make the roof of a house.*

Inside an island home

This home is on one of the islands of Fiji, in the Pacific Ocean. It belongs to the chief of the village. It is decorated with special patterned cloths and white shells.

▼ *The mats on the floor have been made from local grasses.*

This family home is in Japan. The walls are made from light **bamboo** wood and thin **rice paper**. The floors are covered with mats made from straw.

▲ *The family sits on the floor around a low table to eat a meal.*

The weather

Islands around the world have different kinds of weather. Greenland lies in the north of the Atlantic Ocean where the weather is cold. There is snow and ice all the year round.

▼ These homes are in Greenland. You can see ice floating on the water in the bay.

There are hundreds of small islands in the Caribbean Sea. These islands are hot and sunny. Every year from June to November there is the danger of **hurricanes**. A hurricane is a fierce storm with very high winds and heavy rain.

Island life

In 2005, Hurricane Emily damaged over 2,500 homes on the island of Grenada in the Caribbean.

▲ A hurricane has damaged these homes on the Caribbean island of Jamaica.

The environment

Over many years the **sea level** around an island will change. When the sea level falls you can see more of the **sea bed** around the island. When the sea level rises, water covers more of the land and the island gets smaller.

▼ *These homes are in Tuvalu in the Pacific Ocean. If sea levels rise, Tuvalu could disappear beneath the water.*

On some islands there are **volcanoes**.
When a volcano **erupts**, hot rock,
called **lava**, flows onto the land around it.
In 1995, a volcano on the island of
Montserrat erupted. The main town on
the island was covered with lava.

▲ Lava has almost
completely covered
this building on
Montserrat, in
the Caribbean.

School and play

On small islands where there are not many people, school classes may have only a few pupils. If an island is close to the mainland, children may have to travel to the mainland to go to school.

▼ A teacher talks to her pupils in the Cook Islands in the Pacific Ocean.

Children who live on small islands often play on the beach and in the water. They learn to fish and to swim. Sometimes they learn to sail a boat, or to dive down under the water to look at beautiful fish or **coral reefs**.

Island life
The most popular sport in the Caribbean islands is **cricket**.

▲ Children play football on Kuta Beach in Bali in Indonesia.

Going to work

Fishing is important for island people. Sometimes fishermen sell the fish they have caught to local shops and restaurants. Often the fish are taken to other countries to be sold.

▼ These fishermen in the Seychelles have caught lots of fish in their nets.

Warm islands, such as the Caribbean or Hawaii, are popular places for people to go on holiday. Many island people work in hotels or restaurants that are visited by **tourists**.

▲ *This woman sells her baskets to tourists on the island of Fiji in the Pacific Ocean.*

Getting about

On islands such as Great Britain, it is easy to travel around. There are good roads, railways and airports. Greenland is covered with ice and snow, so there are no railways and not many roads. People use helicopters and planes to travel between towns.

▼ People go on a small plane to get to the mainland of Scotland from the island of Barra.

People who live on small islands often use boats to travel to other islands, or the mainland. **Ferries** take passengers as well as cars and other **vehicles** from one island to another.

▲ This ferry travels from the mainland of Goa in India to islands in the Mandovi river.

Where in the world?

Look at these two pictures carefully.

- How are the homes different from each other?

- What is each home made of?

- Look at their walls, roofs, windows and doors.

- How are these homes different from where you live?

- How are they the same?

GREENLAND

ICELA

NORTH AMERICA

ATLANTIC OCEAN

Hawaiian Islands

Caribbean Islands

PACIFIC OCEAN

SOUTH AMERICA

Outer Hebrides, Scotland

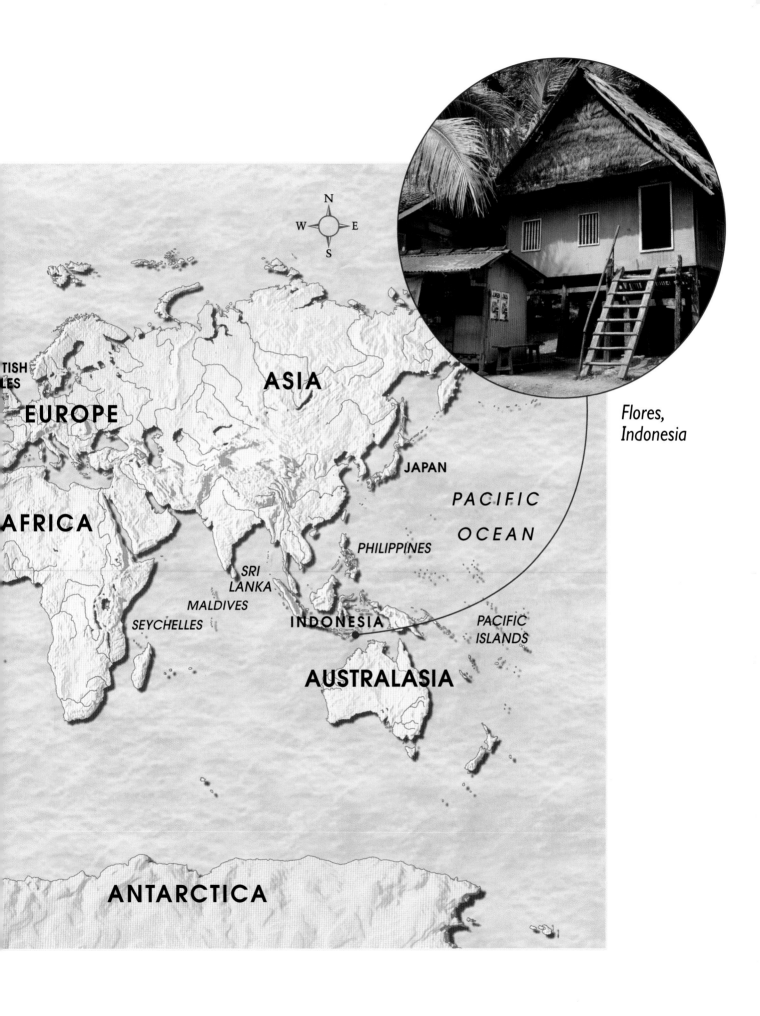

TISH
LES

EUROPE

ASIA

AFRICA

N
W ⊕ E
S

JAPAN

PACIFIC

OCEAN

PHILIPPINES

SRI
LANKA

MALDIVES

SEYCHELLES

INDONESIA

PACIFIC
ISLANDS

AUSTRALASIA

ANTARCTICA

*Flores,
Indonesia*

Glossary

bamboo	a kind of tree
brick	a hard block of mud and sand that is used for building
concrete	a mixture of cement, sand and water that gets harder as it dries
coral reef	a hard, rocky material in warm seas made from the bodies of small underwater creatures
cricket	a sport played between two teams with a small, hard ball and a wooden bat
erupt	when hot rocks are pushed violently from deep below the ground up to the earth's surface
ferry	a boat that carries people and vehicles from place to place
hurricane	a fierce storm with high winds and lots of rain
lava	hot rock that comes out of a volcano
local	near to home
mainland	a large piece of land, rather than the islands around it
material	what something is made of
rice paper	paper that is made from rice
sea bed	the bottom of the sea
sea level	the level of the sea around the world
square kilometre	the area covered by a square measuring a kilometre on each side
steel	a kind of metal that is very strong
stilts	poles that are used to raise something off the ground
tourist	a person who is on holiday
vehicle	any kind of transport with wheels, such as a car or a truck
volcano	a place where lava erupts from deep beneath the earth

Further information

Books to read

Geography First: Islands Christopher Durbin, Wayland (2004)

Starters: Homes Rosie McCormick, Wayland (2003)

My World of Geography: Islands Vic Parker, Heinemann (2005)

Landforms: Volcanoes Acorn Books (2006)

Curriculum Focus – Geography: Islands and Seasides David Flint, Hopscotch Educational Publishing (2003)

Websites

http://www2.hawaii.edu/~ogden/piir/
Pacific Islands Internet resource

http://www.greenland-guide.gl/
The official guide to Greenland

http://www.netstate.com/states/intro/hi_intro.htm
Information about Hawaii

http://www.japan-guide.com/list/e1000.html
Information about the geography of Japan

Index

All the numbers in **bold** refer to photographs.